Animal Sculpture

**Susan Canizares
Pamela Chanko**

**Scholastic Inc.
New York • Toronto • London • Auckland • Sydney**

Acknowledgments
Literacy Specialist: Linda Cornwell
Early Childhood Consultant : Ellen Booth Church

Design: Silver Editions
Photo Research: Silver Editions
Endnotes: Sabrina Jones
Endnote Illustrations: Ruth Flanigan

Photographs: Cover: Niki de Saint-Phalle/*Blue Animal*/Bridgeman Art Library International, Limited; p.1: Karl Ciesluk/*The Quarry Fish*/SuperStock; p. 2: Lawrie Simonson/*The Ladybird*/Bridgeman Art Library International, Limited; p. 3: Deborah Butterfield/*Rex*/The Lowe Art Museum/SuperStock; p. 4: Karl Ciesluk/*Glass Fish*/SuperStock; p. 5: Anonymous/photo by Remi Benali/Gamma Liasion; p. 6: Anonymous/Private Collection/Dean Fox/SuperStock; p. 7: Clark Coe/*Killingworth Image Man on a Hog*/National Museum of American Art/Art Resource; p. 8: Anonymous/SuperStock; p. 9: Anonymous/*Bottlecap Lion*/National Museum of American Art/Art Resource; p. 10: Salvador Dali/*Telephone-Homard*/Christie's Images/SuperStock; p. 11: Niki de Saint-Phalle/*Blue Animal*/Bridgeman Art Library International, Limited; p. 12: Ann Duncan/photo by Ken Karp

No part of this publication may be reproduced in whole or in part, or stored in a retrieval system, or transmitted in any form or by any means, electronic, mechanical, photocopying, recording, or otherwise, without written permission of the publisher. For information regarding permission, write to Scholastic Inc., 555 Broadway, New York, NY 10012.

Library of Congress Cataloging-in-Publication Data
Canizares, Susan, 1960-
Animal sculpture / Susan Canizares, Pamela Chanko.
p. cm. -- (Learning center emergent readers)
Summary: Presents different animal sculptures and their materials,
including a rock fish, metal horse, and wooden pig.
ISBN 0-439-04594-0 (pbk. : alk. paper)
1. Sculpture--Juvenile literature. 2. Animals in art--Juvenile literature.
[1. Sculpture. 2. Animals in art.]
I. Chanko, Pamela, 1968- . II. Title. III. Series.
NB1143.C36 1998

731.832--dc21   98-48700
                                                                                                                              CIP AC

Copyright © 1999 by Scholastic Inc.
Illustrations copyright © 1999 by Scholastic Inc.
All rights reserved. Published by Scholastic Inc.
Printed in the U.S.A.

Rock fish.

Metal ladybug.

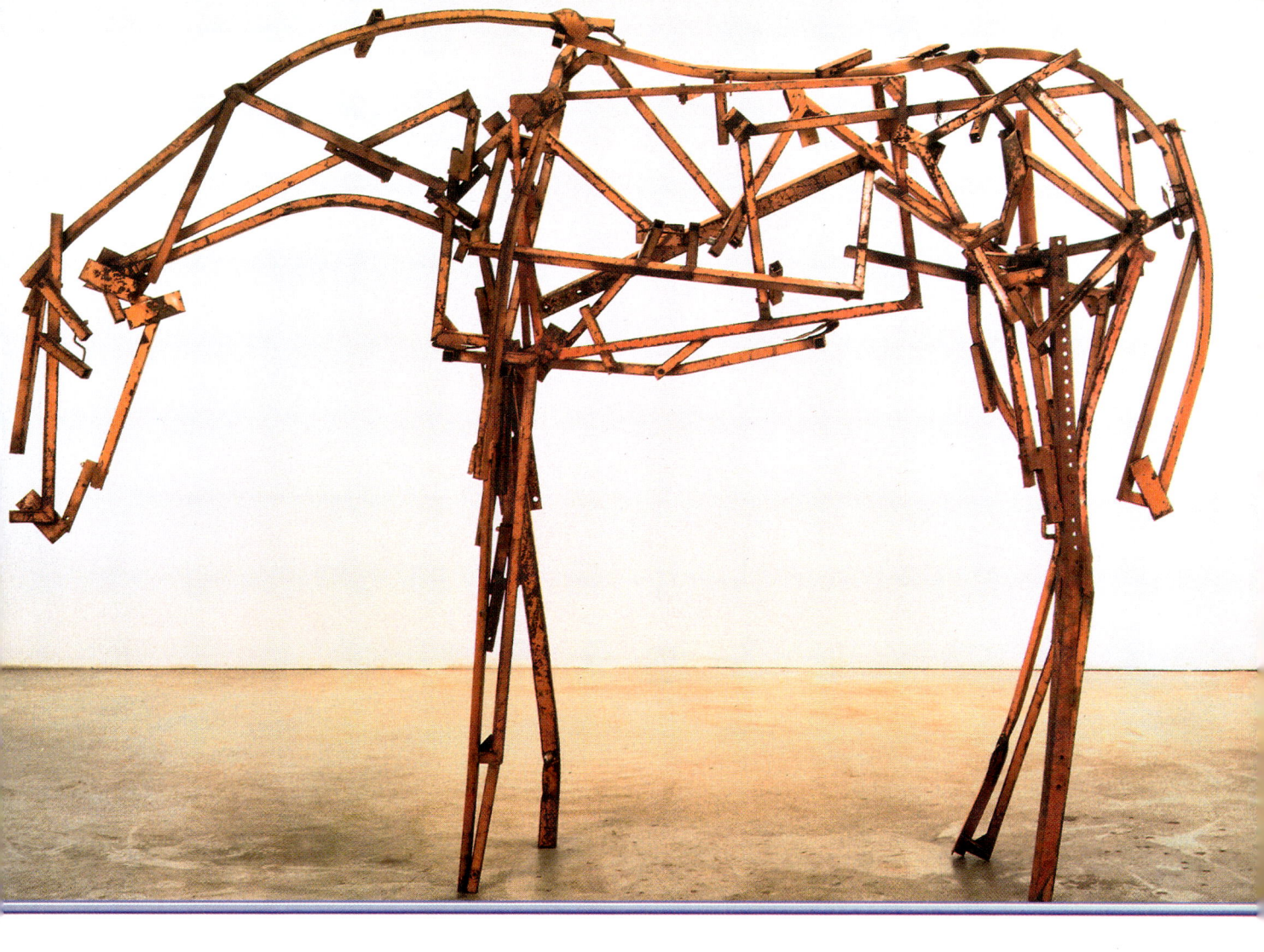

Metal horse.

Glass fish.

Ice birds.

Wooden dog.

Wooden pig.

Paper frog.

Bottle-cap lion.

Plastic lobster.

Plastic donkey.

Pineapple porcupine!

Animal Sculpture

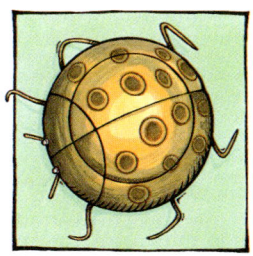

A sculpture can be made out of anything. Some sculptors use traditional materials, such as wood, clay, and metal. Others also borrow tools and materials from building construction, the kitchen, and even the trash. Animals are great subjects for sculpture. Each kind has its own special characteristics.

Rock fish This is *Two Quarry Fish* by Karl Ciesluk. The fish look like they are swimming in the water that reflects their lower halves. The artist built them out of rocks in a natural environment. He put them here because fish live in water and also because this water is in a quarry, a place where the rock is cut from the ground.

Metal ladybug This is *The Ladybird* by Lawrie Simonson. To make this sculpture, she cut sheets of metal for the body, and rods for the legs and antennae. Then she heated them with a gas torch so she could bend them into shape. The metal was polished to make a shiny shell like a real insect.

Metal horse This is *Rex* by Deborah Butterfield. Scraps of pipe and hardware are normally used in buildings and machines. This artist put them together to make a life-sized horse. The pieces are connected with strong beads of melted metal, called welds.

Wooden dog This sculpture was made by an anonymous artist. This means that the name of the artist is unknown. He or she carved the ears with a knife, found a stick for a tail, and stuck them in holes in the head and body. Then the face and spots were painted on. This dog looks like a good jumper!

Wooden pig This is *Man on a Hog* by Clark Coe. He built it the way a carpenter would make furniture. The bodies are made of boards, cut and nailed together. The heads are carved and the pig's ears are cut out of tin. The skin is painted. Scraps of cloth tell us the rider used to have clothes. The sculpture is very old, over a hundred years, and the fabric has worn away.

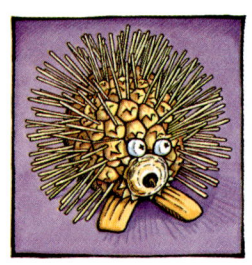

Glass fish This is *Glass Fish* by Karl Cieseluk. It is another kind of fish in water, different from the rock fish we saw earlier. This time the artist has taken broken pieces of glass and glued them together. Light shines through it, just like the water that reflects its lower half.

Ice birds This sculpture was carved from a big block of ice for a festival on a frozen river. Ice festivals are popular in cold northern states where rivers and lakes stay frozen for many months. To carve these birds, the artist started with a chain saw for the big shapes. Then the details were chipped out with a chisel. Sometimes the tools are heated to melt the ice.

Plastic lobster This is *Telephone-Homard* by Salvador Dali. He took two familiar things, a telephone and a lobster, and put them together in a surprising way. It is the artist's idea that makes art out of these store-bought items. How would you like to hold a lobster up to your ear?

Plastic donkey This is *Blue Animal* by Niki de Saint-Phalle. First she made a hollow mold in the shape of the animal. Then she filled it with plastic resin. She poured the mixture into the mold, where it hardened into a strong sculpture.

Paper frog This frog was folded from a single square of colored paper. No cutting was involved. In the Japanese art of origami, you can make many kinds of animals by following traditional patterns or by making up your own folds.

Bottle-cap lion Making animals out of bottle caps is a good way to recycle! To make this lion, the caps were strung on wires and wrapped around a frame of wood and plastic. Think of all the things you throw away that you could make into sculptures!

Pineapple porcupine Ann Duncan raided the refrigerator to make this pineapple porcupine with toothpick quills and marshmallow and clove eyes. He won't last as long as most sculpture does, but he is a lot of fun. How would you like to meet him on your dinner table?